THE CHESTER COUNTY
HISTORICAL SOCIETY

PETER BERWIND SCHIFFER

PUBLISHED BY WHITFORD PRESS
Exton, Pa. 19341

Library of Congress Card No. 70-184722

FIRST PRINTING: December 1971

PRINTED BY TINICUM PRESS
West Chester, Pennsylvania 19380

Peter B. Schiffer attended Franconia College and graduated from Goddard College. He taught credit courses for two years on American Decorative Arts as an undergraduate. He has been in the antique business (Herbert Schiffer Antiques, Inc.) with his father since he was 17. Soon they will publish "American and English Miniature Furniture" and a third book, also a joint effort, "19th Century Chinese Porcelain for the American Market."

Mr. Schiffer's mother is Margaret B. Schiffer, author of "Chester County Furniture and Its Makers" and "Historical Needlework of Pennsylvania". A third, "Chester County Architecture" is at the printers.

ACKNOWLEDGEMENTS

I would like to thank the past and present staff of the Chester County Historical Society, Philip Holmes, my college advisor, and my father and mother for their interest and encouragement with my thesis which is the basis of this book.

PETER BERWIND SCHIFFER

CHESTER COUNTY, PENNSYLVANIA

It was William Penn's plan for Pennsylvania that it should be a "Holy Experiment" where men would have the opportunity to make a new start in the world. In 1667 Penn had formally joined the Friends, generally called Quakers, and in 1681 he had written: "After many waitings, watching, soliciting, and disputes in council my country was confirmed to me under the great seal of England. God will bless and make it the seed of a nation." To this territory was given the name of Pennsylvania. A number of settlers, mainly Dutch, Swedes, Finns and English, had been living in the newly formed territory of Pennsylvania, for some years, among the American Indians. These settlers lived for the most part near the Delaware River, the Schuylkill River and tributary creeks.

William Penn, who was a skillful organizer anxious to convert his wilderness into productive land, set about publicizing the advantages of his colony to Englishmen, Germans, Frenchmen and Dutchmen. Through pamphlets and other publications, especially in Germany, the news was quickly circulated that a new land had opened, flowing with opportunity and productivity, where both political and religious liberty were promised.

Three main motivating forces influenced the different religious, ethnic and national groups that contributed to the settling of Pennsylvania: the desire for religious freedom, relief from political persecution and economic advantages.

Chester, Philadelphia and Bucks were the three original counties to be formed in 1682 in Pennsylvania by William Penn, under Charter signed by King Charles II. The county was named for Chester in England from which some of the first settlers had come. In the beginning Chester County extended westward from Philadelphia County. In 1729 part of the western section of Chester County was organized as Lancaster County, and in 1789 the south-eastern townships were organized as Delaware County. Chester County's southern boundary is the Mason-Dixon Line, laid out in 1763, and the unique circular boundary separating Pennsylvania from the state of Delaware.

The greatest number of settlers to Pennsylvania after 1682 came from the British Isles. It was quite natural that the majority were Quakers. Penn had a concern for the establishing of a haven of refuge for the Friends in the New World. Not all of these were English. The so-called Welsh Barony was settled by Welsh Quakers. It included the townships of Haverford, Radnor, Merion, Tredyffrin, Whiteland, Easttown and Goshen.

During the first decade of the eighteenth century there was a great influx of Irish Quakers who were chiefly of English origin but had lived in northern Ireland for over a generation.

The Germans, beginning in 1683, arrived in Pennsylvania and spread out quickly into the country outside the periphery of early English Quaker settlements. Germany at this time was a collection of principalities each with its own ruler and a state religion. There was little sympathy for dissenters, and furthermore the entire country was suffering from the ravages of the Thirty Years War. A religious movement known as Pietism had swept Europe. The German sects produced by Pietism had much in common with Quakers. By 1730 many of the Germans, the so-called Pennsylvania Dutch, had settled in the northern townships of Coventry, Vincent, Pikeland and Nantmeal. Besides the plain sects, some were members of the Lutheran, Reformed and other German churches.

From the early eighteenth century many Scotch-Irish Presbyterians and Welsh Baptists settled in both the Great Valley and the southwestern section of the county. A few French Huguenots and Roman Catholics also settled in the county.

The first year for which complete tax assessment lists for the county have survived is 1715. Eight hundred seventy-seven taxables are listed for that year. This increased to 2,229 in 1735, 5,089 in 1760 and 5,942 in 1775. These figures from the tax assessment lists indicated heads of families plus unmarried males of legal age.

The first United States Federal Census was taken in 1790, just one year after Delaware County was formed from the southeastern part of Chester County. This census shows a total of 4,454 families comprising 7,939 individuals. The rapid growth of the population of the county is reflected in the following figures from the Federal Census: 1800: 32,093, 1810: 39,595, 1820: 44,451, 1830: 50,910, 1840: 57,515, and in 1850: 66,438. The black population is included in the above figures; it increased from 688 in 1790 to 5,523 in 1850.

For over two hundred years the population of the county was primarily rural, conservative, and middle class with a strong Quaker element. In 1683 the plough was the leading device on the official seal. Even though there was a constant flow of settlers westward, most families found in eighteenth century tax assessment lists were still to be found in the same township in 1850. Although the county was primarily agricultural it did not have a purely rural culture. The Quakers went to Philadelphia for Yearly Meetings and also to market where they had the opportunity for seeing city styles which they could adapt to their own taste.

An exception to this primarily agricultural economy was the establishment of iron forges and furnaces beginning about 1718. This industry still flourishes with iron and steel mills principally in Coatesville and Phoenixville.

Today United States Routes 1, 30 and 202 cross the county.

William Penn's belief in Pennsylvania became a reality.

By the time of the American Revolution, Philadelphia was the second largest city in the English speaking world and until about 1840 Pennsylvania was known as the "bread basket of America."

This combination of opportunity and political and religious freedom to men from various nations unknown in the Old World made Pennsylvania also America's first melting pot.

CHESTER COUNTY HISTORICAL SOCIETY

There has been an active interest in the history of Chester County and its people from the first quarter of the nineteenth century. The first published effort was probably "Letters on the History of Chester County" by Joseph J. Lewis (1801-1883). This was published in the Village Record, in West Chester, in 1824.

Dr. William Darlington (1782-1863) followed in the foot steps of Humphrey Marshall, of Chester County, who in 1785 had published "Arbustum Americanum". Dr. Darlington commencing in 1826 published many works on Chester County botany. Extant are several manuscript compilations containing Chester County documents found in county and state archives. Just before his death he published in the Village Record, in West Chester, "Notae Cestrienses" which appeared between 1860 and 1862.

The first major printed book was "History of Chester County, Pennsylvania, with Genealogical and Biographical Sketches" published in 1881 by J. Smith Futhey and Gilbert Cope. Beginning in 1861 Mr. Cope compiled many genealogies and local history items. He was probably the leading spirit of the thirty-six men and four women who affixed their signatures in 1893 to the application for the charter of the Chester County Historical Society. The purpose of the Society was "the acquisition and preservation of property and information of historic value or interest to the people of Chester County."

Dr. Joseph T. Rothrock, the eminent conservationist sometimes known as "the father of forestry in Pennsylvania", was elected as the first president. He was followed in 1894 by Dr. George Morris Philips, in 1920 by Judge J. Frank E. Hause, in 1928 by J. Carroll Hayes, Esq., in 1937 by Dr. Francis Harvey Green, in 1951 by Dr. Arthur E. James and in 1967 by George Norman Highley.

The headquarters of the Chester County Historical Society, at 225 North High Street, West Chester, was built in 1848 for the Chester County Horticultural Society. The architect was Thomas U. Walter, who had previously designed the Methodist and Presbyterian Churches, Cabinet Hall, the Bank of Chester County, the West Chester Young Ladies Seminary, the Court House, Prison, the Market House office, Judge Bell's house at 101 South Church Street, the Misses Price's School on West Union Street, the addition to the David Townsend House and perhaps Mayfield in West Chester. Thomas U. Walter is perhaps more famous as the architect for the wings and dome of the Capitol in Washington, D. C., the Preston Retreat and Girard College in Philadelphia. His skill as an architect in the Greek Revival style caused West Chester to be called "The Athens of Pennsylvania".

In 1880, Uriah H. Painter purchased Horticultural Hall at a Sheriff's sale for $2000. Extensive alterations and additions transformed it into "The West Chester Opera House" seating 420 people on the main floor and 180 in its suspended gallery. For the next fifteen years the Opera House was a center for theatrical entertainments and social or cultural activities.

In 1904 the widow of Mr. Painter deeded the Opera House to the General George A. McCall Post, Grand Army of the Republic, with the stipulation that it was to become the property of the Chester County Historical Society when the Civil War Veterans no longer wished to use it. At this time the building officially became known as "Memorial Hall".

In 1936, when the McCall Post no longer needed the building it was acquired by the Chester County Historical Society. Price and Walton, Philadelphia architects, were engaged to draw plans for adapting the building for museum and library use and to design a three-story, fire-proof library addition. On February 28, 1942 the Chester County Historical Society had a formal opening of the building.

The Society normally holds public meetings on the third Tuesday of each month from September through May. Talks, frequently illustrated, of historic interest are presented. Over the years various aspects of local history, from the days of the Lenape Indians to the recent past have been discussed by speakers.

Another contribution of the Society has been the marking for posterity of historical landmarks in the county. Through its efforts places as the Star Gazers' Stone of Mason and Dixon fame, the birth places of authors and scientists, and similar sites have been marked.

The Society also publishes pamphlets and brochures from time to time.

All persons interested in the history of Chester County and its people are invited to become members. Contributions of an historic or genealogical nature to the library, museum or museum houses are also welcome and, incidentally, are tax deductible, as are legacies or bequests in wills.

Through all of these varied activities the Chester County Historical Society is accomplishing its chartered purpose:

"the acquisition and preservation of property and information of historic value or interest to the people of Chester County."

THE LIBRARY

The library, located at 225 North High Street, in West Chester, includes not only printed and published source material, but also an extensive clipping file from county newspapers and a large collection of manuscripts.

Books, newspapers, pamphlets, broadsides, maps, and pictures are all included in the file of printed material. These include not only standard works on the history of Pennsylvania and its counties and books on early industry, antique glass, furniture, silver, ceramics and other Americana, but also a collection of the works, regardless of subject, by Chester County authors.

The clipping file contains material from the early nineteenth century to the present and is being added to continually. Every aspect of the history of the county and its people is represented.

The local newspaper files are particularly extensive, dating from 1808 to the present, while the collection of almanacs date from 1719. Genealogical data in the library files pertain not only to Chester County but also to southeastern Pennsylvania and adjoining sections of Delaware, Maryland and New Jersey as well.

The manuscript collection includes county tavern records; tax assessments; deeds; court, school, and church records. There are also miscellaneous account books, diaries, family letters, genealogies, marriage certificates, Bible records, minute books of organizations, and military records invaluable to researchers.

THE MUSEUM

The collections of the Society are on exhibit in the Main building, 225 North High Street, West Chester, in the Brinton 1704 House, Birmingham Township, in the David Townsend House, West Chester and in the Hopper House in East Whiteland Township.

In the main building there are room arrangements of William and Mary, Queen Anne, Chippendale, Classical and Windsor furniture. The special study collections include Majolica, Tucker, Canton, pottery, delft and other ceramics, glass, lighting fixtures, silver, iron, tin, pewter, needlework, particularly local samplers and needlework accessories, wearing apparel, textiles, coverlets, quilts, pictures by local artists, dolls, paper dolls, toys, minerals and Indian relics. There are also a carpenter shop, shoemaker and saddler shop, blacksmith shop, pottery, a country store, country kitchen and school room.

The Brinton 1704 House is furnished with furniture and accessories used in the county before 1751 when William Brinton, the builder, died. In the barn there are vehicles, farming utensils and implements, basketry and farm and out kitchen utensils.

The David Townsend House contains furniture and accessories of the Classical and Empire periods.

The Hopper House is furnished primarily with nineteenth century furniture.

Brinton 1704 House, south front

1704 BRINTON HOUSE

Oakland Road, Birmingham Township

William Brinton, Jr. came from Staffordshire England to Birmingham Township, Chester County, in 1684 with his parents. For twenty years they lived in a plank house, twenty-one by twenty-five feet, on the plantation. In 1704 William Brinton, the son, built a two and a half story quarried stone house known as "William Brinton's Great House". The house is twenty-two by forty feet.

The basement consists of a kitchen and two small cellars. On the first floor there is a large hall and parlor chamber. By 1750 the second floor had been divided into an entry and three chambers. There is a large unceiled attic with five sloping dormer windows.

Among the interesting architectural features of the house are the steep roof, the high stone chimneys topped out with brick, the steeply sloping shed dormers, ceiled and unceiled penteaves, leaded glass casement windows, benches

Brinton 1704 House, basement kitchen

Brinton 1704 House, first floor hall

on either side of the front door, a water table and a large stairway directly to the basement kitchen. The kitchen has a flag stone floor, candle niche, and an inside bake oven. The first and second floor fire places have raised hearths and the rooms are divided by walnut partitions. The house has an unusual number of large closets most of which have a window and grill work over the doors. The ceilings of the first and second floors are plastered and the staircases between the floors are lighted by small windows.

The furnishings of the 1704 Brinton House are based on inventories taken during the 1750's when William Brinton and his wife died.

Brinton 1704 House, second floor chamber

Collins Mansion, south front

COLLINS MANSION

Goshen Road, West Goshen Township

Joseph Collins built the first section of this stone house in 1727 in West Goshen Township. Over the hood of the front door is a date stone inscribed I $\begin{smallmatrix} C \\ M \end{smallmatrix}$ for Joseph and Mary Collins. Above the door there is a cantilevered hood. On the Collins Mansion the projecting hood is used with a pent roof, the beams of the main room of the house projecting thru the walls to support the pent eave and hood. The original house is two and a half stories high, twenty-three by twenty-one feet, facing south. The front facade is built of dressed serpentine stone, from a local quarry, and the sides are built of field stone. Serpentine stone, of distinctive green color is found in the county. The roof has a steep pitch and is today covered with composite shingles. Originally there were on the south front four leaded sash casement windows, with small fixed sash above.

Inside the Collins Mansion the first floor consisted of one room with a large cooking fireplace. The stairway to the second story was in the northwest corner. The second floor had a passage hall with two rooms separated by a poplar board partition. The attic was one large unceiled room. By 1760 Nathaniel Moore added a field stone kitchen, twenty-five by twenty-three feet, to the original house. At this time the former kitchen fireplace was removed from the original house and a small "parlour" sized chimney was erected on the original supporting arch.

Collins Mansion, first floor parlor

David Townsend House, west side

THE DAVID TOWNSEND HOUSE
225 North Matlack Street, West Chester

The David Townsend House takes its name from David Townsend, its owner from 1849 to 1858, banker, botanist, and prominent West Chester citizen. The house was built in three sections; the first about 1790, the second section in 1830, and the final section by David Townsend in 1849.

The name of the builder and the exact date of construction of the original section of the house are not known. The house was in a traditional square style, one and a half stories high, with a cellar. On the ground floor there was only one large room originally, with a stairway to the second floor. There were two smaller rooms on the second floor, In 1830 a brick addition of two and a half stories was attached to the south end of the original building. There is a possibility that Thomas U. Walter was the architect. This 1830 section has been changed but little since it was added, with its wide hall through the house and the two rooms to the west. Sometime before 1874 the roof was raised to present three-story level.

David Townsend House, first floor parlor

David Townsend House, first floor dining room

David Townsend House, third floor Victorian parlor

In 1849 David Townsend purchased the house and moved his family into it to make it his residence. Shortly after this purchase the third section was added to the house, Townsend employing a Thomas Bateman to attach a brick addition thirty-one feet by sixteen feet to the eastern wall of the north wing of the building. "The said Thomas," the agreement read, was "to find all the materials and labor and finish the said building in a plain and substantial manner."

The entrance hall, parlor and dining room on the first floor, and the three bedrooms on the second floor have been furnished with Heppelwhite and Sheraton furniture. Ceramics, pictures, needlework and other accessories are appropriate for the period.

The two rooms and hall on the third floor have been furnished as a parlor and bedroom with Empire and Victorian furniture.

Hopper House, east side

Hopper House Barn

17

William and Mary Walnut Wainscott Chair

WAINSCOT CHAIRS
WITH CHESTER COUNTY CREST RAIL

Chairs of this type are among the earliest survivals in the Delaware Valley and seem almost medieval in design. The chair incorporates almost all the decorative devices employed by local chairmakers at the end of the seventeenth century; vigorously turned front posts and stretcher, kept within the plane of the block; shaped and scored arms with graceful under cutting; molded seat frame usually made to receive a cushion; semi-circular tops to rear posts; recessed or raised back panel; and an elaborate crest consisting of a central fan and two horns. This particular cresting has been found on numerous chairs made by unknown Chester County joiners. In order of frequence the primary woods for chairs of this type are walnut, oak and cherry. More arm chairs have been found thus far than side chairs. Some chair backs have inset balusters below the crest rail.

William and Mary Walnut Gate-leg Table

William and Mary Walnut Blanket Chest

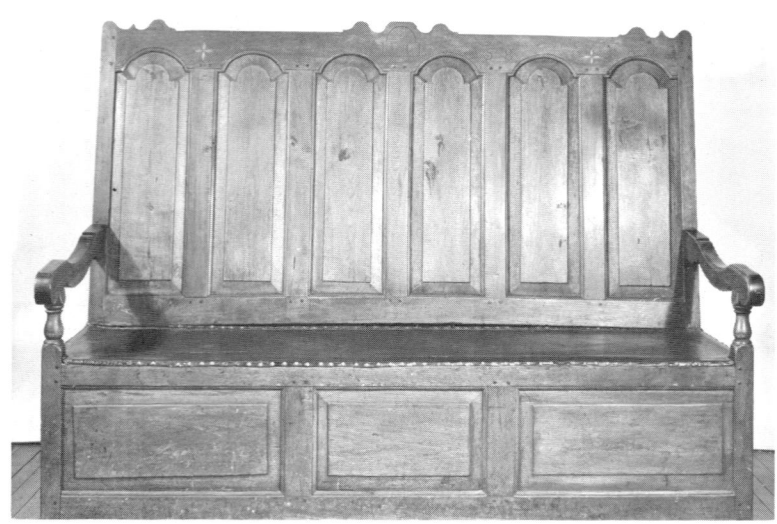

William and Mary Walnut Settle dated 1758

20

CHESTER COUNTY INLAY

This distinctive incised decoration of volutes and berries is the most usual form of inlay found in Chester County. Tulips, figures of humans and birds were employed and herringbone or simple line inlay was used to outline drawers and case pieces. Both dates and family initials were delineated in simple line inlay. The forms discovered, thus far, with this mode of decoration include chests of drawers, blanket chests, tables, clock cases, dressers, chairs, settles, sampler frames, clothes presses, corner cupboards and spice, Bible, hat and document boxes. Dated pieces range from a 1706 William and Mary chest of drawers to an 1820 classical table. Walnut is the usual primary wood while the inlay is done with holly, cherry, putty, pewter, or brass. Most of the pieces of furniture apparently originated in southern and southwestern Chester county.

Detail of line and berry inlay

Queen Anne Walnut Chest of Drawers
and
William and Mary Walnut Bible Box

Queen Anne Walnut Tall
Case Clock by Benjamin Chandlee

Queen Anne Walnut Tall
Case Clock by Isaac Thomas

ROUND BIRD CAGE STANDS AND TABLES

Candlestands and tea tables with snake feet, cabriole legs, depressed ball or bulbous post turnings, birdcage and dish tops, were popular for a long period. A Chester County cabinetmaker in the Downingtown area in the second half of the eighteenth century has here added a distinctly local touch — a circular birdcage with either three or four posts. Tea tables with the same birdcage are known. The tables differ only in size and to use, and vary in quality of execution. Each table found has been of walnut.

Chippendale Walnut Candlestand

Painted Slat Back Chairs

Queen Anne-Chippendale Transitional Walnut Chairs

25

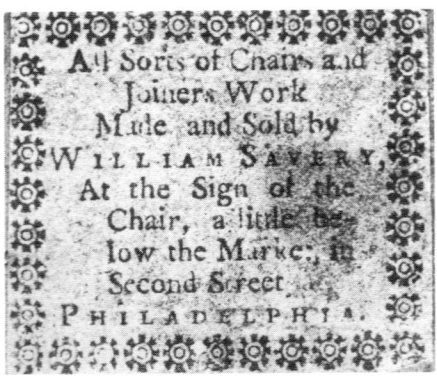

Queen Anne Walnut Slant-lid Desk, with William Savery label

Chippendale Walnut Slant-
lid Desk and Book Case

Chippendale Walnut
Chest on Chest

27

Detail of interior

Chippendale Octorara Walnut Slant-lid Desk

28

OCTORARA DESK

The Octorara desk is a distinctive local form found along the creek of this name which forms the western boundary of Chester County. The typical desk has these special features: high, full ogee feet with a closed circle cut out, plain (rather than reeded or fluted) quarter columns, and so-called "pen" or "candle" drawers for the fall front writing surface usually made of oak with a facing (these facings each contain an intaglio carved pinwheel), shaped interior drawers, pigeon hole side panels, and shell carved pigeon hole drawers and central door. The desks are usually of walnut with oak, pine and poplar as secondary woods.

High chests of drawers, usually of walnut, having the plain quarter column and the high ogee foot with a closed circle cut out, two of the Octorara characteristics are known. Less frequently chests on chests, clothes presses and blanket chests are found.

Classical Walnut Chest of Drawers. Label of Isaac Weaver.

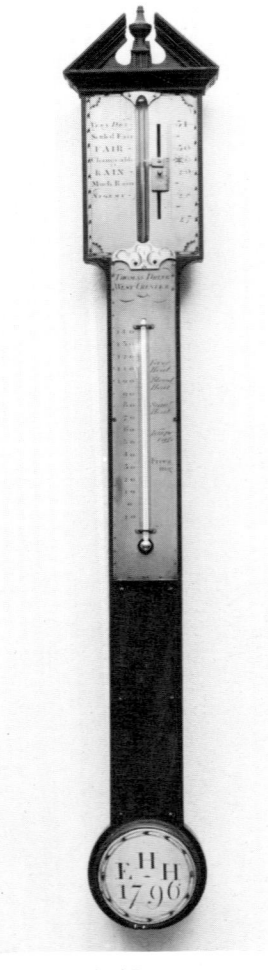

Classical Barometer
made by Thomas Dring

Chippendale Walnut Screen

WINDSOR CANDLE STANDS

This product of a local turner is the county's contribution to the field of windsor furniture. Windsor candle stands have circular tops supported by three turned legs and braced by three turned stretchers. They average twenty-five inches in height, and the circular dish top averages seventeen inches in diameter. The turnings vary from the bold windsor turnings of 1760-1770 to the bamboo turnings of about 1800. The earliest candle stands found are constructed of walnut or butternut wood and were not painted. Later ones were made of soft woods, had bamboo turnings, and were painted either red or green.

Windsor Butternut Candlestand   Windsor Painted Candlestand

Windsor Painted Bow Back Chairs. Label of Samuel Moon

Windsor Painted Arrowback Chairs. Label of Joseph Jones

SPICE BOXES

Spice boxes were made in Chester County from the end of the 17th century to the early part of the 19th century, and consequently the same motifs employed by the cabinetmakers on their full size furniture were used on these diminutive case pieces. They were used to hold small articles of value such as silver spoons, silver and gold buttons and silver banded pin cushions. Spice boxes rest on ball feet, bracket feet (straight, cut out, full ogee and French) or on frames with trumpet turned, Spanish, pointed slipper, or claw and ball feet. All local spice cabinets have a door with lock. Sometimes only the door has inlaid decoration, in other instances this inlay is also found on the sides, interior drawers and rather seldom on the top. The "secret" compartment when found in spice boxes is in the cornice, in the back panel or in back of front drawers. One spice box with quarter columns and one with a bow front are known. The woods employed were walnut, cherry, mahogany, apple, maple, cedar, poplar and butternut.

William and Mary Walnut Inlaid Spice Box

Queen Anne Walnut Inlaid Spice Box

34

Queen Anne
Walnut Spice Box on Frame

Chippendale
Walnut Spice Box on Frame

EARTHENWARE

Pottery is an ominbus word which is used to describe everything which is not porcelain. Earthenware is opaque ware which is porous after the first firing, and which must be glazed before it can be applied to domestic use.

Earthenware was found in most homes in the county until about 1850. It was used for plates, mugs, basins, bed pans, crocks, jugs, jars, bowls, pots, dishes, cups, pans, chambers, pitchers, moulds, pipkins, hanging baskets, spittons, vases, stove pipes, collars, water pipes, tiles, toys, banks, flower pots, etc. The inventories taken at the time of a person's death, during the seventeenth century mention treen, pewter and earthenware. In the eighteenth century delftware, pewter and earthenware are listed for table use and in the nineteenth century Queensware becomes popular.

The majority of potteries were working between 1750 and the time of the Civil War and the period of industrialization. Most of the early potteries were operated on a part time basis. The men were farmers or tradesmen as well as "Bluebird potters".

Redware, stoneware, brownware, Rockingham ware and yellow-ware are the various types made by the local potters. Some of the families engaged in the industry continued working over several generations.

Earthenware Toy

Earthenware Funnel, Stove Support, Gigging Light and Shaving Mug

Earthenware Turk's Head, Bean Pot and Bed Pan

Earthenware Mid-drip Candlestick   Earthenware Flower Pot made
by John Vickers and Son

Stoneware Water Filter, Chicken Fountain and Jug

DELFT

Delftware is a fairly soft earthenware covered with a glaze of lead made opaque with ashes or oxide of tin. On this white absorbent surface the decorator painted his pattern or picture swiftly and irrevocably, as though he were working in water color. The family of tin glazed earthenware is large. Its history begins, not, as is often thought, with the Netherlands town of Delft, but in Moorish Spain and Renaissance Italy. Through Majorca — so acquiring the name maiolica, or majolica — there came into Italy shipments of magnificent wares with lustred and other decoration which caught the imagination of Italian potters inspiring them to make similar wares in their own styles. From Italy the art of majolica spread through Europe. In German, France and other northern countries it became known as faience or fayence. What we now call "delftware" was made in England and Flanders before it was made in the town of Delft, Holland. During the seventeenth and eighteenth centuries the delft potters attempted to copy the popular, yet expensive, Chinese Export porcelain which was being imported from China.

The Society has in its collection plates with cobalt blue decoration dated 1738 and bearing the initials of men and women who lived in southern Chester county. The plates are believed to have been made in Bristol, England.

Delft Plates made for the Dixon, Allen, Beverly and Gregg Famililes

Porcelain made at the Vickers Pottery

TUCKER CHINA

Tucker china, manufactured in Philadelphia between 1825 and 1838, was one of the first porcelains to be made in America.

Benjamin Tucker was proprietor of a china store at 324 High Street, in Philadelphia. His son, William Ellis Tucker, became interested in decorating some of the imported white china which was sold in the shop. A small kiln was erected at the back of the store, but it was not financially profitable.

In the early 1820's Israel Hoopes, of New Garden Township, Chester County, discovered kaolin, a white china clay, on his farm. In later years the Tucker family purchased land in Chester County to obtain the kaolin.

By 1826 William E. Tucker had sufficient funds to start manufacturing chinaware at the Philadelphia Water Works, 23rd and Chestnut Streets and started to produce Tucker china. He had many technical difficulties but by 1827 William Tucker received honorable mention and a citation of merit from the Franklin Institute for the best "porcelain either plain white or gilt, made in Pennsylvania."

By 1828 Thomas Hulme, of Philadelphia, had invested money in the business. For about eighteen months the business was known as "Tucker and Hulme". The majority of pieces closely resembled imported china and were purposely unmarked so that it could be sold as imported china. In 1828 Thomas Tucker, brother of William "commenced to learn the different branches of the business . . . by serving several years apprenticeship."

The financial difficulties continued but finally the interest of Judge Joseph Hemphill was aroused and he invested money in the firm for his son Alexander. At this time a considerable factory was erected at Chestnut and Schuylkill Sixth (now 17th Street) which was to become a show place for visitors to Philadelphia.

The partnership of Tucker and Hemphill had been in existance less than two years when William Tucker died on August 22, 1832. The following year Judge Hemphill paid $10,000 for Tucker's interest in the business. He also employed Thomas Tucker as Factory manager and took his son, Robert Coleman Hemphill into the business. It was Thomas Tucker who painted many of the bouquets and garlands of flowers and some of the little landscapes, particularly the Philadelphia views, all of which are so typical of Tucker China.

The great bank failure of 1833 again led to financial difficulties. Joseph Mariner, of Boston, bought the china factory and all the equipment and real estate for $40,000 but it would seem that the kilns were never fired. In 1837 Thomas Tucker took a six months lease on the factory. In 1852 he wrote he "continued the business for some time until I filled the store with porcelain of my own manufacture of porcelain and commenced ordering from Europe." The wheel had made full circle and Tucker had a china shop again which featured European imports.

Tucker china is found undecorated and decorated with sepia and charcoal landscapes, with gold, with gold and buff, with gold and polychrome, with gold and polychrome flowers, with gold and polychrome landscapes, with gold and polychrome sprigs, with gold landscapes and with gold and polychrome special subjects. Known forms made include tea and dinner sets, garnitures, vases, urns, pitchers, ink wells, perfume bottles, baptismal bowls and toys.

Tucker Grecian, Vase and Walker Type Pitchers

Part of a Tucker Tea Set

Staffordshire Plate marked
"Wm Everhart Importer WEST CHESTER" and "J. Holden"

43

Tucker Baptismal Bowl dated 1834

MAJOLICA

Majolica is the term applied to cream colored earthenware with a lead or tin glaze, stained with coloring oxides to produce brilliant effects. The Majolica derives from a type of ware made in Marjorca, Italy from the fifteenth century. In France it was known as Faience and in Holland as Delft.

In 1882 the first Etruscan majolica was made at the Phoenixville Potteries, Starr and Church Streets, Phoenixville, Chester County. Between 1867 and 1882 the potteries had made yellow ware, Rockingham ware, Parian, ornamental terra cotta and cream colored ware. In 1879 the pottery had been leased to Henry Griffin, George Griffin, David Smith and William Hill trading under the name of Griffin, Smith and Hill. The designer was an Englishman named Bourne. It is the monogram of this firm, the intertwining initials G S H, the initials and the words Etruscan Majolica, the word Etruscan, or all three, which identifies majolica ware made in Phoenixville.

Large quantities of Etruscan Majolica was purchased by the Atlantic and Pacific Tea Company to be given away as premiums. Because of this there was a wide distribution of Phoenixville Majolica throughout the United States. Many of the articles were ornamental objects with elaborately modeled designs of animals, fish, vegetables and floral motifs which had to be hand painted.

Among the forms made were tea sets, bowls, pitchers, spittoons and plates.

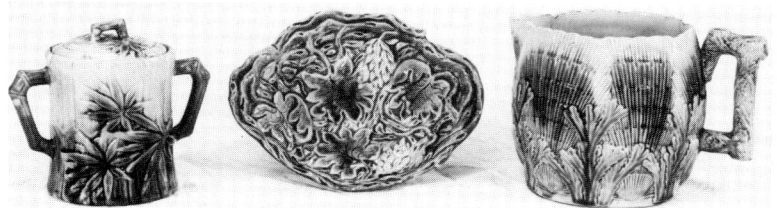

Majolica Sugar Bowl, Dish and Pitcher

Majolica Punch Bowl

PEWTER

Pewter was made of tin and lead. The porportions of each in America varied from pewterer to pewterer. Pewter was in great demand in Chester County during the seventeenth, eighteenth and early part of the nineteenth centuries. The forms used included dishes, basons, canns, platters, plates, pots, spoons, mugs, salt cellars, trenchers, tankards, porringers, quarts, flaggons, bowls, soup tureens, candlesticks, studs and communion sets.

The Society is fortunate to have in its collection a tureen and soup bowl used at the Westtown School and dies and marked porringers made by S. Pennock who worked in the county.

Pewter Bowl and Tureen

47

Pewter Porringer Marked S P for S. Pennock

Pennock Pewter Touches

Iron Franklin Stove signed "MORDECAI PEIRSOL"

Silver Cann made by Joseph Lownes and a
Silver Salver and Tea Pot made by Joseph Richardson

49

Tin Squirrel Cage

Tin Weather Vane

Tin Political Banner made in 1844 by
William and Thomas M. Howard

50

NEEDLEWORK

The Society has one of the outstanding regional collections of needlework and needlework accessories in America. The samplers, canvas work, crewel embroidery, silk embroidery and quilts in the large collection were for the most part made by girls of English Quaker descent.

Among the earliest examples of dated needlework are the men's pocket-books embroidered in Forentine stitch in wool. Many of the pocket-books are both initialed and dated. The dates range from 1751 to 1801.

In Chester County silk was used for many of the most important pieces of needlework. Although stores in the county are known to have sold crewel yarns little crewel embroidery has survived. The Society has a few crewel embroidered pot holders, needlecases, pockets, pictures, etc.

Of great interest is the Society's important collection of local samplers ranging in date from the early eighteenth century through the twentieth century. Included are the school samplers, Dresden, mending and darning, architectural, mourning, map, genealogical, etc.

The Society has an extensive collection of nineteenth century Berlin embroidery. At this period the women also worked bureau covers and bedspreads in trapunto work. The collection of bed coverings is large: woven, patched and appliqued.

Chair Cushion embroidered in tent and cross stitch

Man's Pocket-book embroidered in flame stitch

Dresden Sampler dated 1790

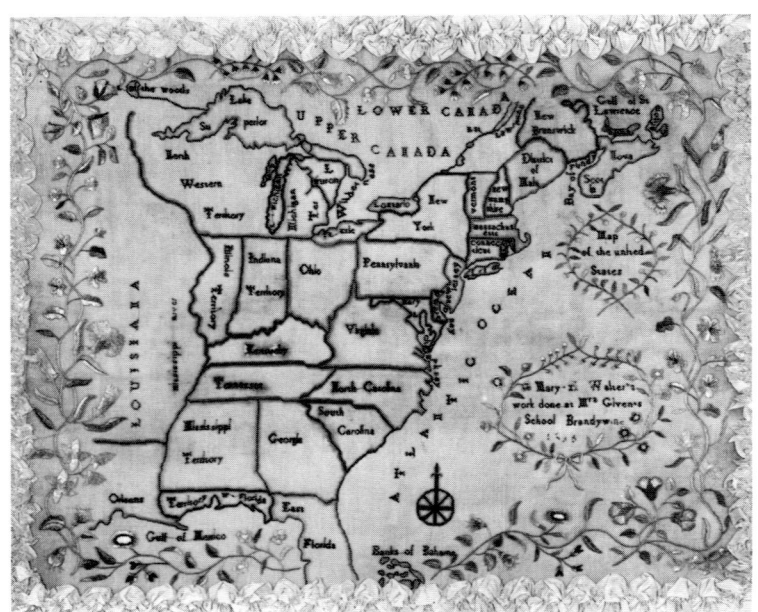

1813 "Map of the United States" worked at Mrs. Given's School

1825 Sampler worked by Sarah Elizabeth Cooper

54

1837 Sampler worked by Mary Caley

Berlin work picture made by Phebe Anne Sharpless in 1850

Crewel work picture inscribed "SARAH HAMPTON ANNO DOMINY 1775"

Patchwork Autograph Quilt signed by Isabelle P. Lukens in 1842 and 1843

Woven Coverlet marked "I M C Windle 1841 C Peterman Brandywine C C Pa."

Book Showing Samples of Textiles Made In the County

Crazy Quilt

Sewing Bird and Pin Cushion

Work Bag and Silver Banded Pin Cushion and Hook

Water Colors signed "Merab Taylor's , Picture. Wrote 3 mo. the 13th 1799"

Water Color Valentine. "A TRUE LOVERS KNOT" of Hannah Matlack

Portrait of Rebecca Webb Baker, wife of Lownes Taylor,
Painted by Bass Otis in 1832

Lancscape Painting of Lownes Taylor's Farm Painted by Bass Otis in 1832

DOLLS AND TOYS

The collection of dolls at the Society is excellent both in its scope as to the period covered and to the materials of which the dolls were made. Wood, china, bisque, rag, composition of all kinds, metal, wax, oil cloth, paper, etc. are all represented. Labeled or marked dolls, especially Greiner dolls with a Philadelphia 1858 patent date, French and German dolls of the last quarter of the nineteenth century and American dolls of 1850 to date are well represented. Dolls made in the local county prison, local Quaker dolls and home and commercially made dolls of local significance are included. There is a large collection of doll clothing. Doll houses with furniture (ca. 1835-1910) and accessories add to the value of this study collection.

Paper dolls and toys are very well represented not only by commercially produced American, English, French and German dolls from 1800 to date, but by hand-made ones of the eighteenth century through World War I. Paper doll houses and furniture, peep shows, hot air paper toys, activated valentines, theatre and miscellaneous toys of the nineteenth and twentieth centuries also contribute to the collection.

Montenari Type Wax Doll

Paper Mache Doll

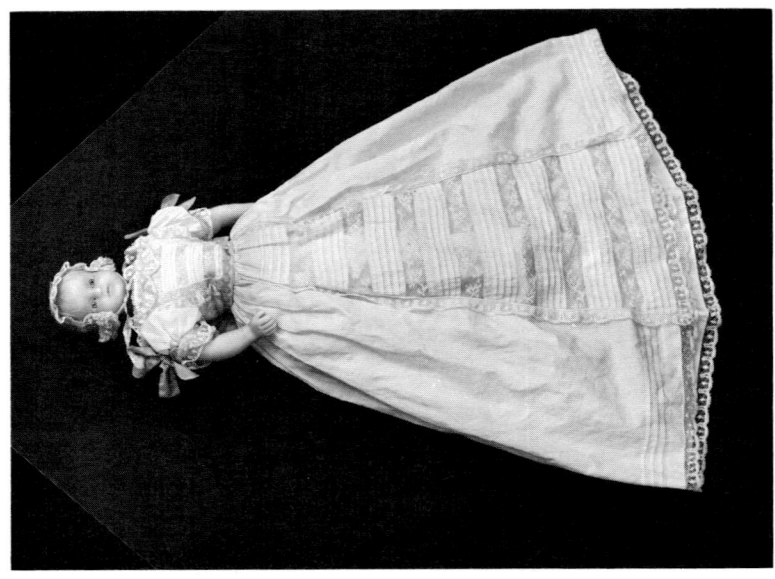

Doll with a china head
and cloth body

Bisque Doll with a
swivel head marked "Depose
Tete Juneau." BTESGDGI"

65

Parlor of an 1836 doll house

Bed room of an 1836 doll house

"LOTTE LOVE" Paper Doll, McLoughlin Bros., N. Y.

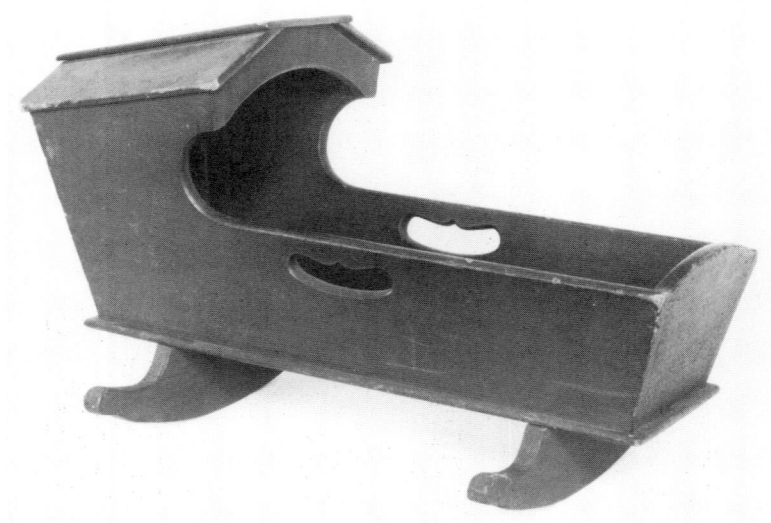

These two pictures are a reminder that the Chester County Historical Society has preserved objects used by residents of Chester County from the cradle (a fine walnut hooded cradle Cira 1760) to the hearse (a horse drawn example) from the large collection of wagons and farming implements in the Brinton 1704 House Barn.

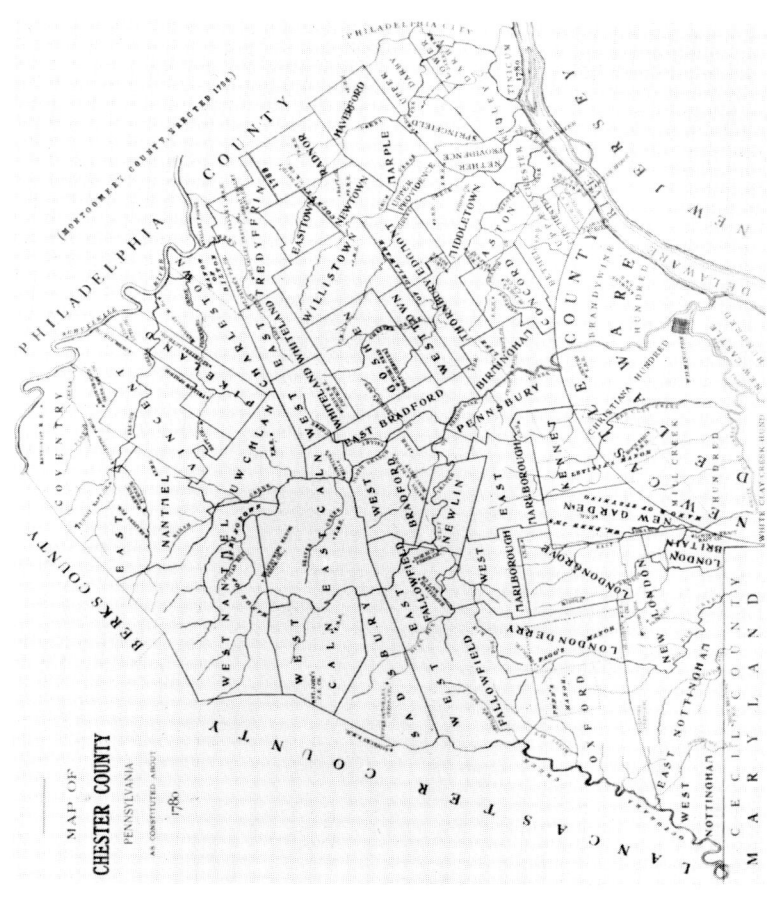

MAP OF CHESTER COUNTY
PENNSYLVANIA AS CONSTITUT-
ED ABOUT 1780. From Gilbert
Cope, *Genealogy of the Smedley
Family*